Intuitive Mandalas

Coloring Book and Journal

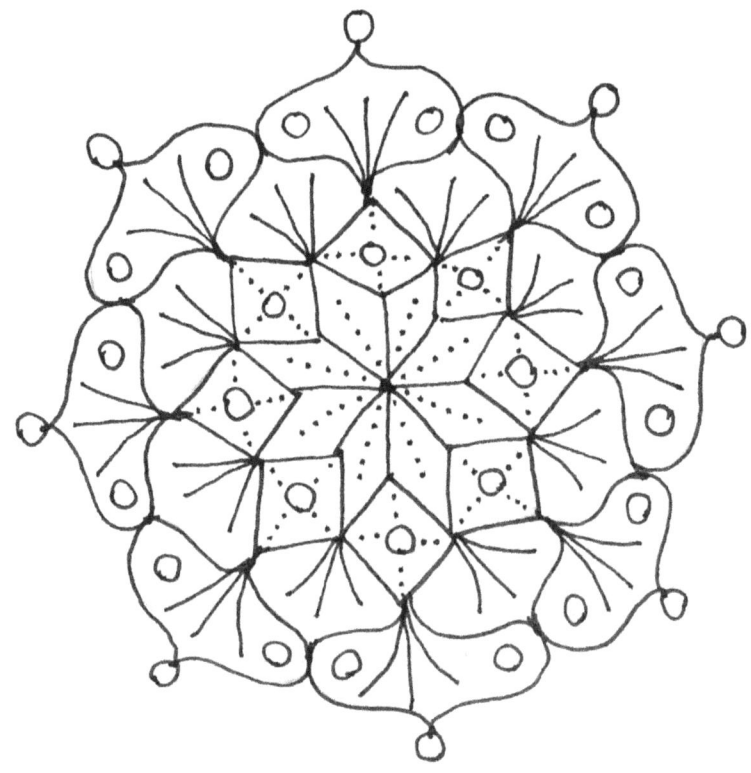

Sami Cave

Copyright © 2020 Sami Cave

All rights reserved. No part of this publication may be reproduced or transmitted in any form, electronic or mechanical, without permission in writing from the author/artist.

A Note From the Author

A mandala is essentially a circle and in Hindu and Buddhist traditions it represents the universe. I have been drawing mandalas for the last four years as a meditative practice. Each one tells a story and even in coloring them I receive intuitive insights that help me.

The journal lines provide a place to capture any thoughts, ideas or insights that appear while coloring and/or meditating on the mandalas.

May these mandalas inspire you as much as they did me. I am grateful to be able to share them with you.

Sami

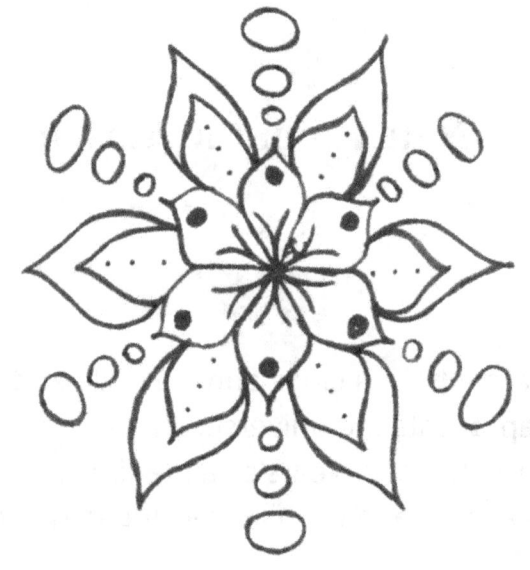

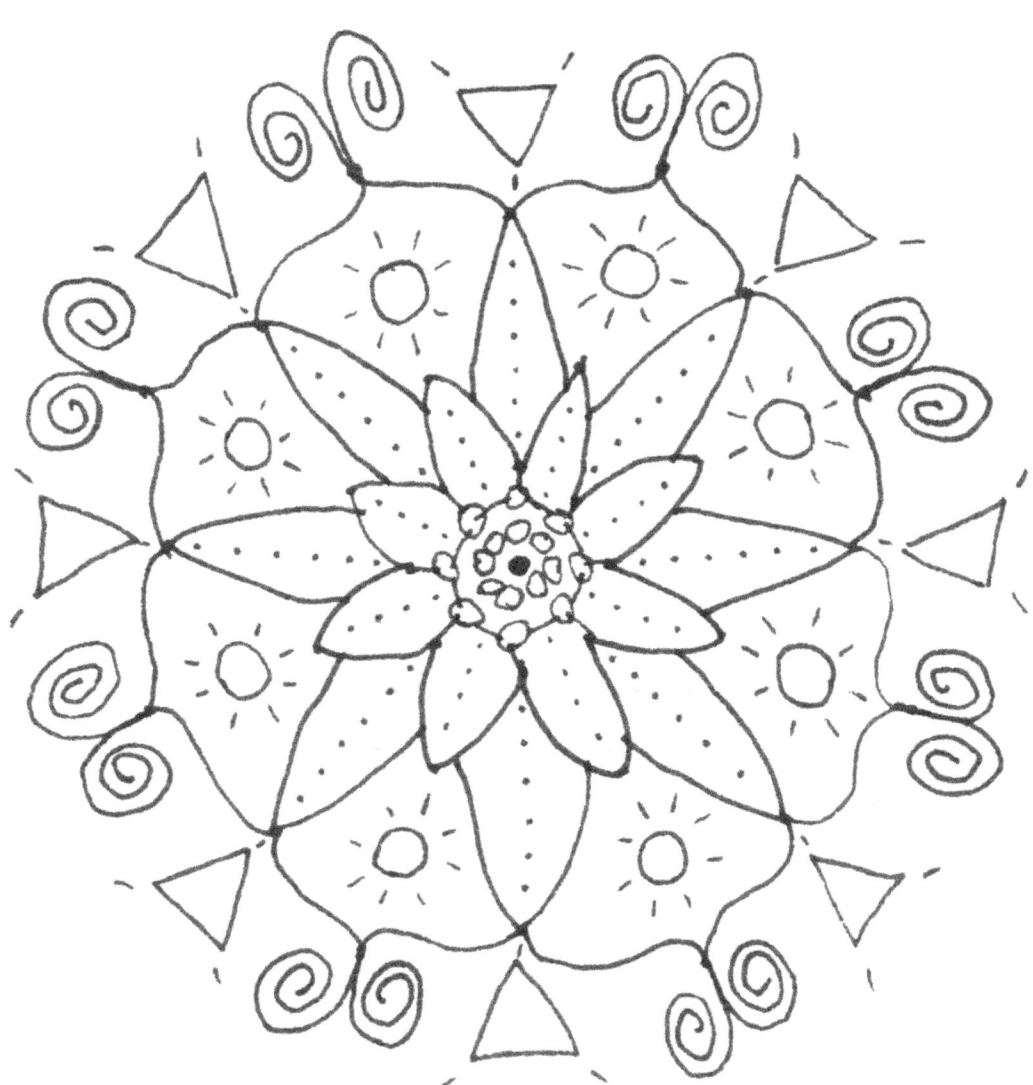

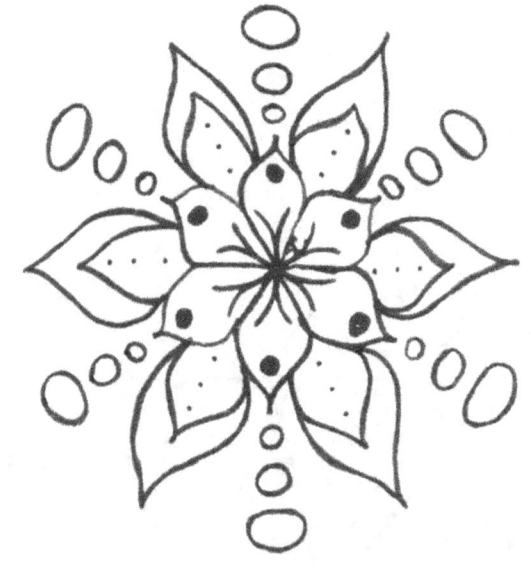

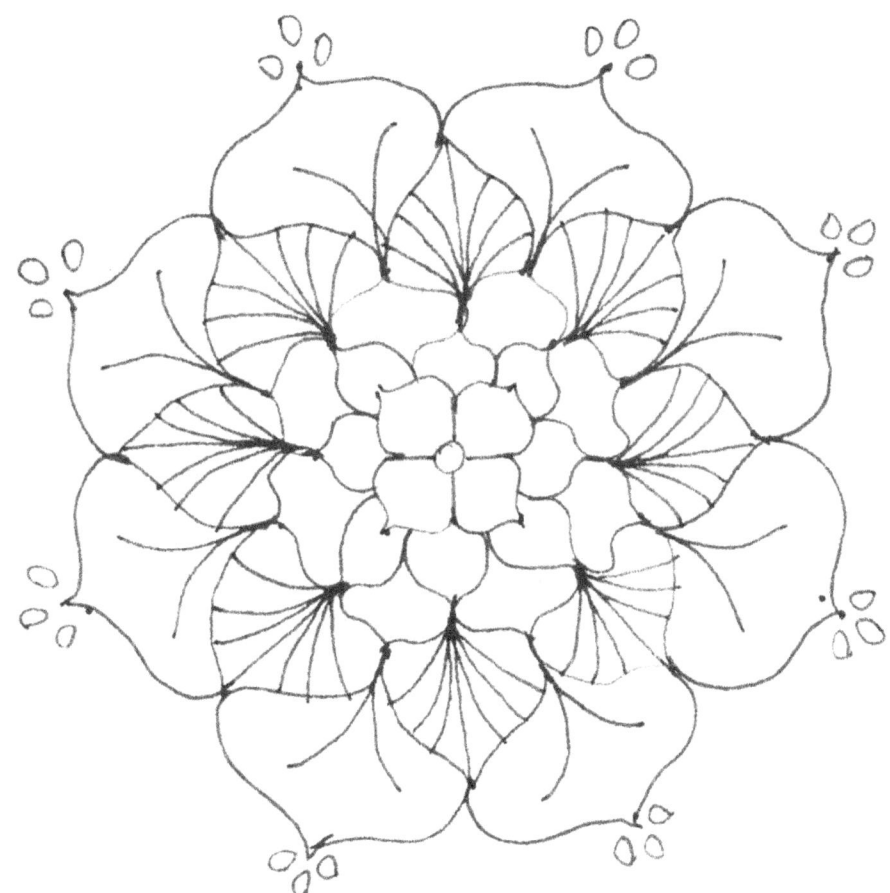

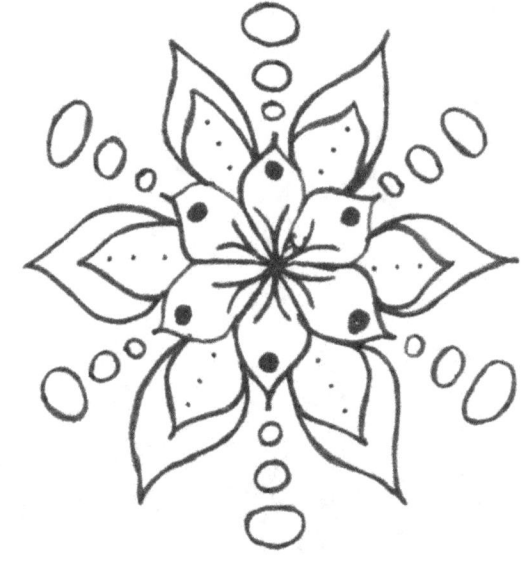

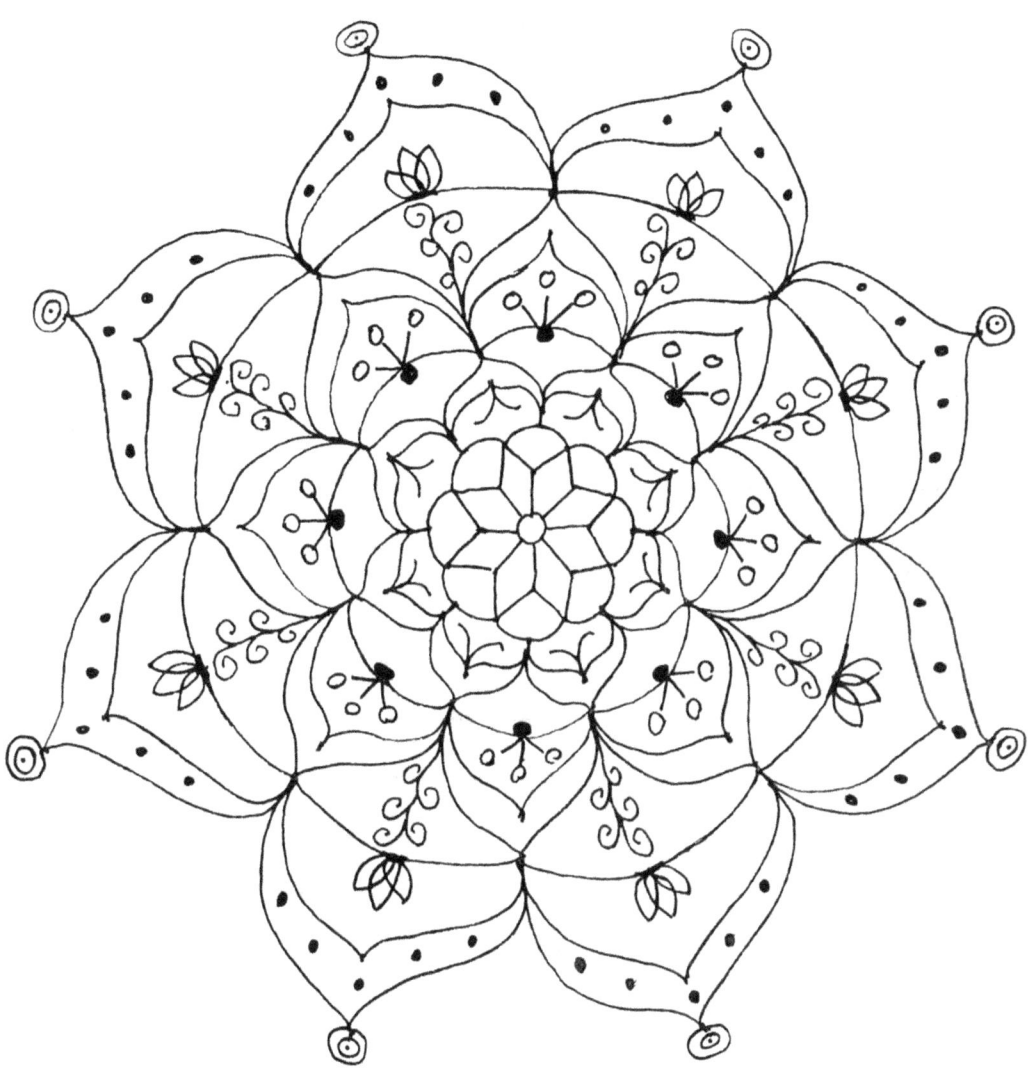

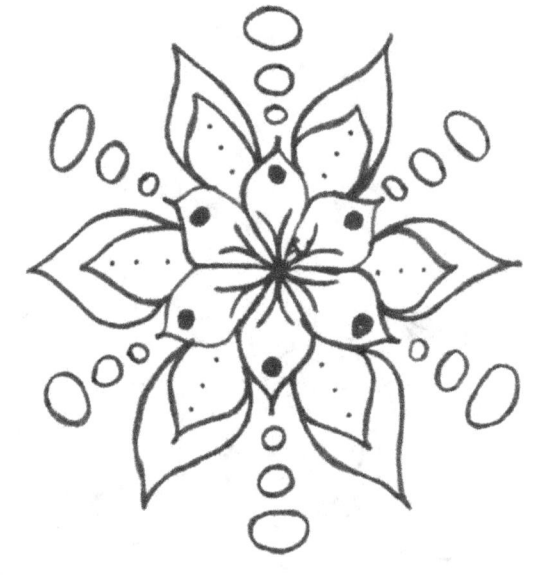

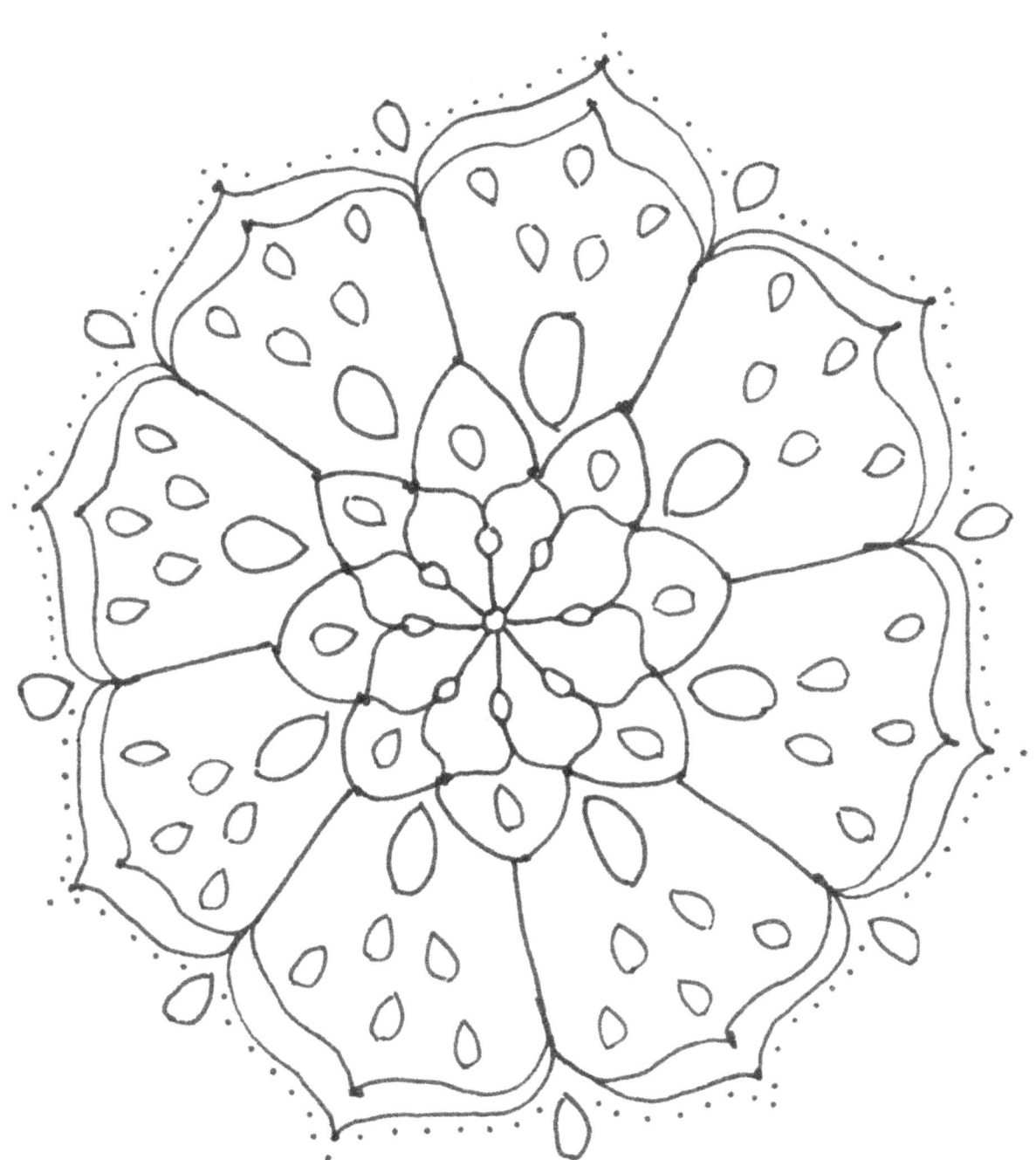

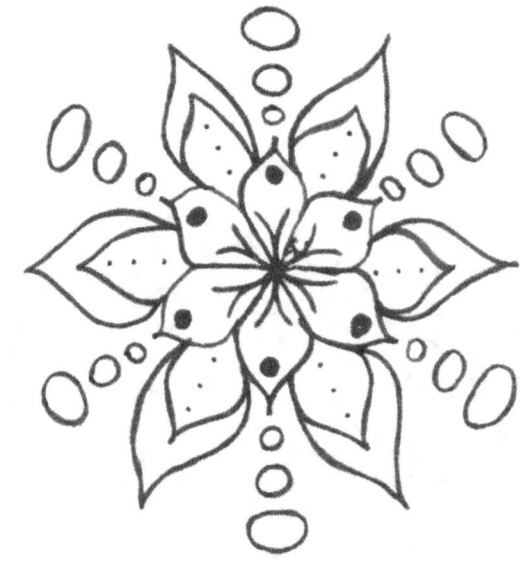

_____
_____
_____
_____
_____
_____
_____
_____
_____
_____
_____
_____
_____
_____
_____

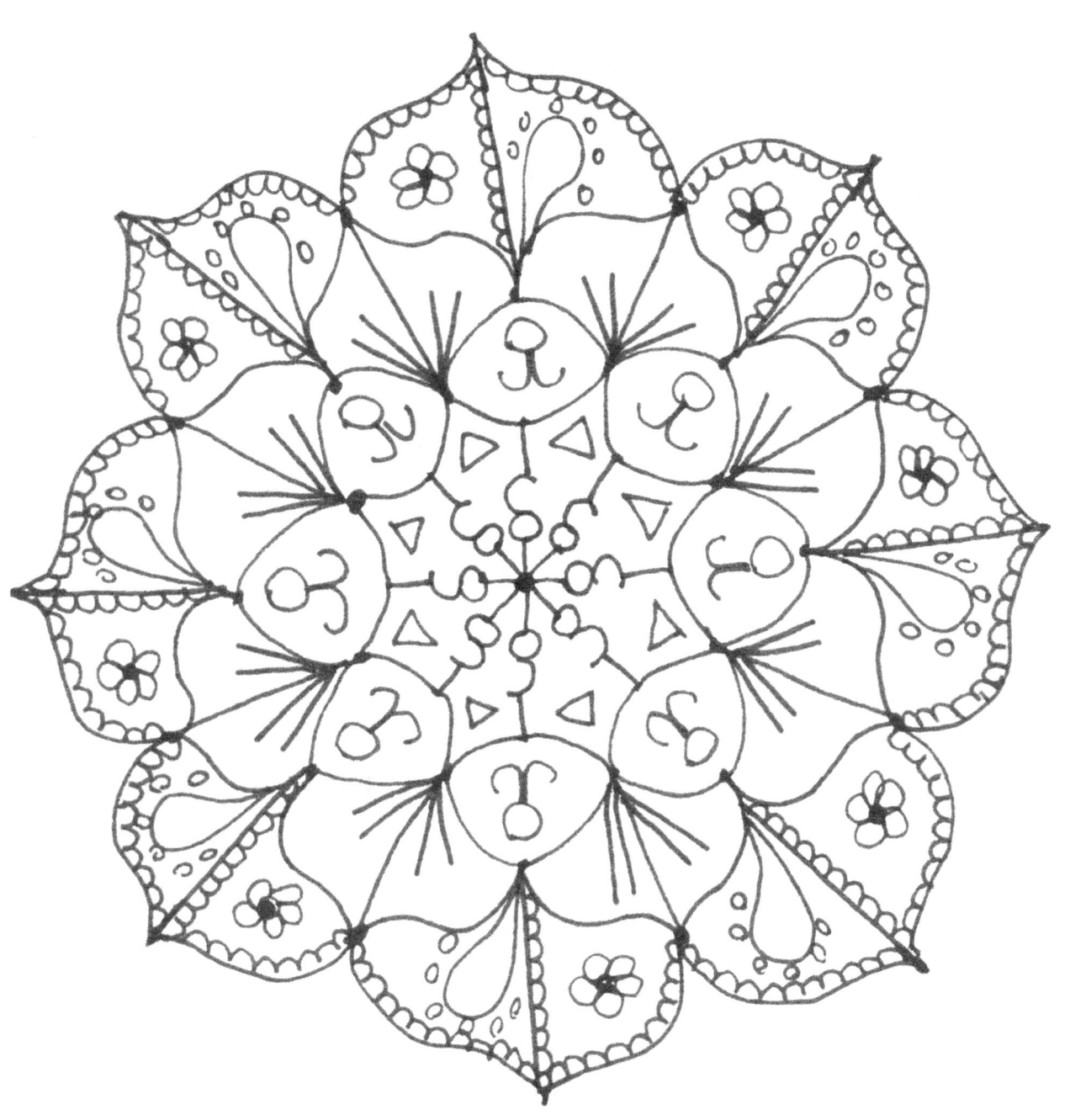

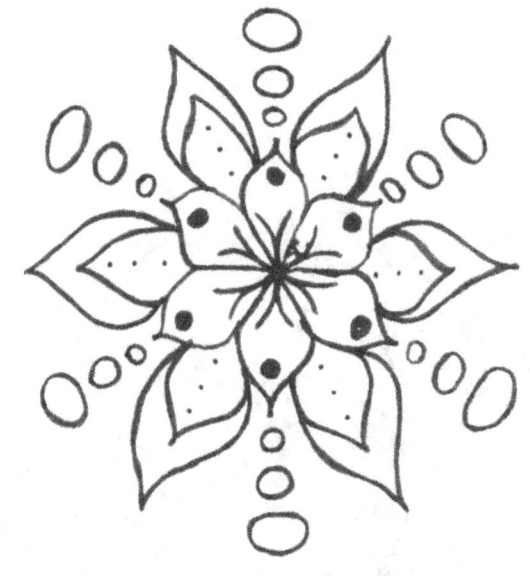

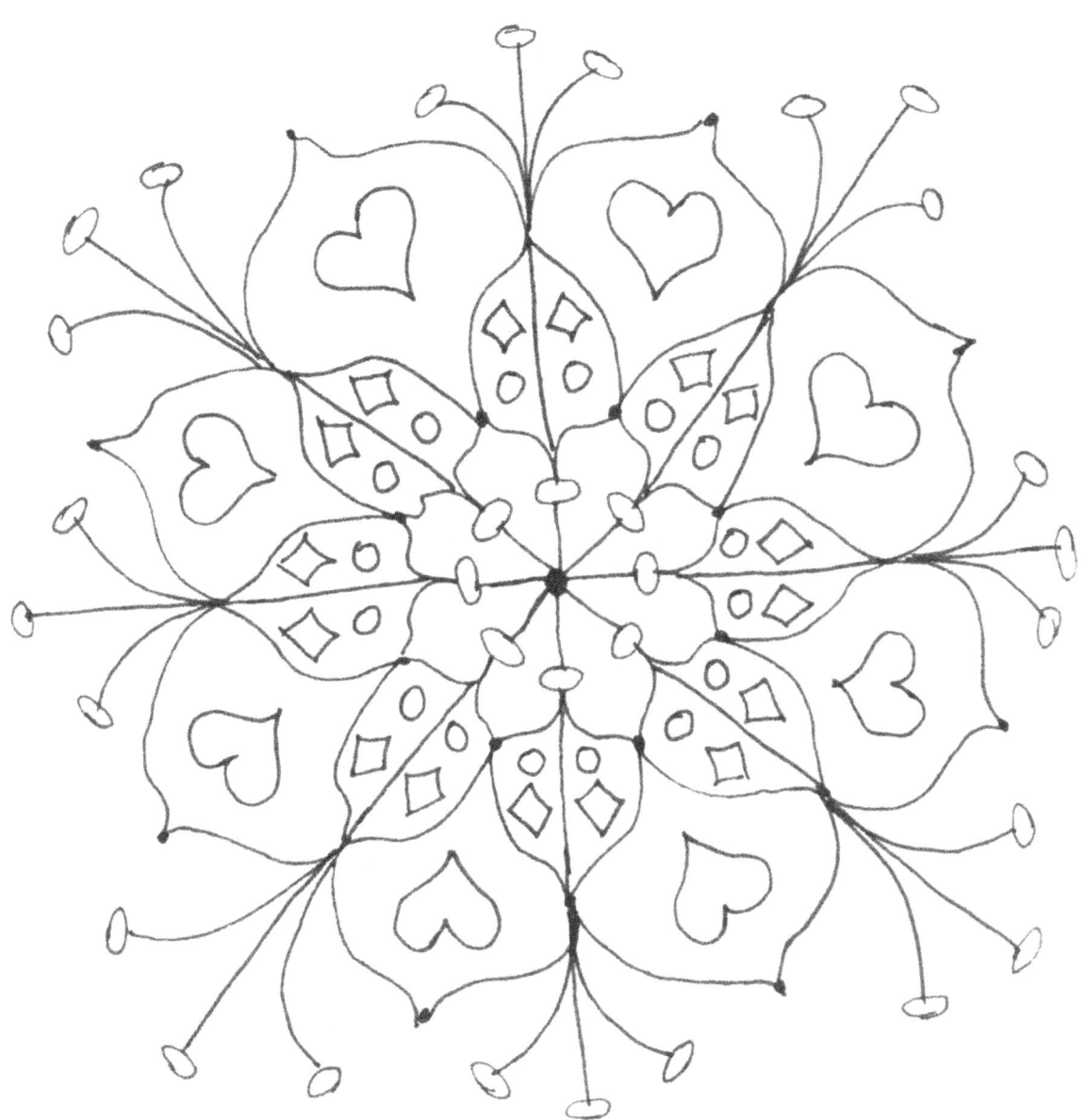

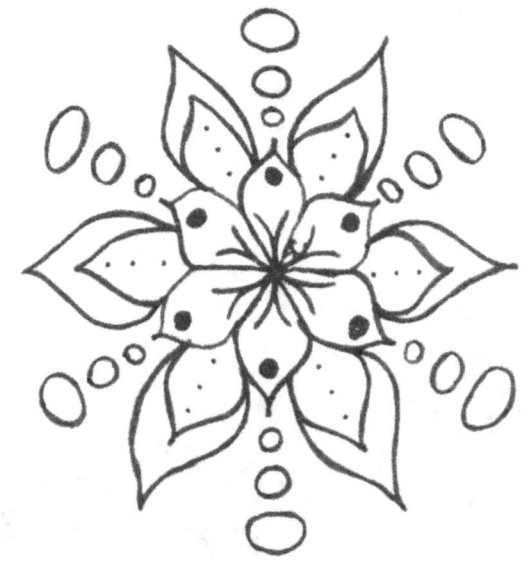

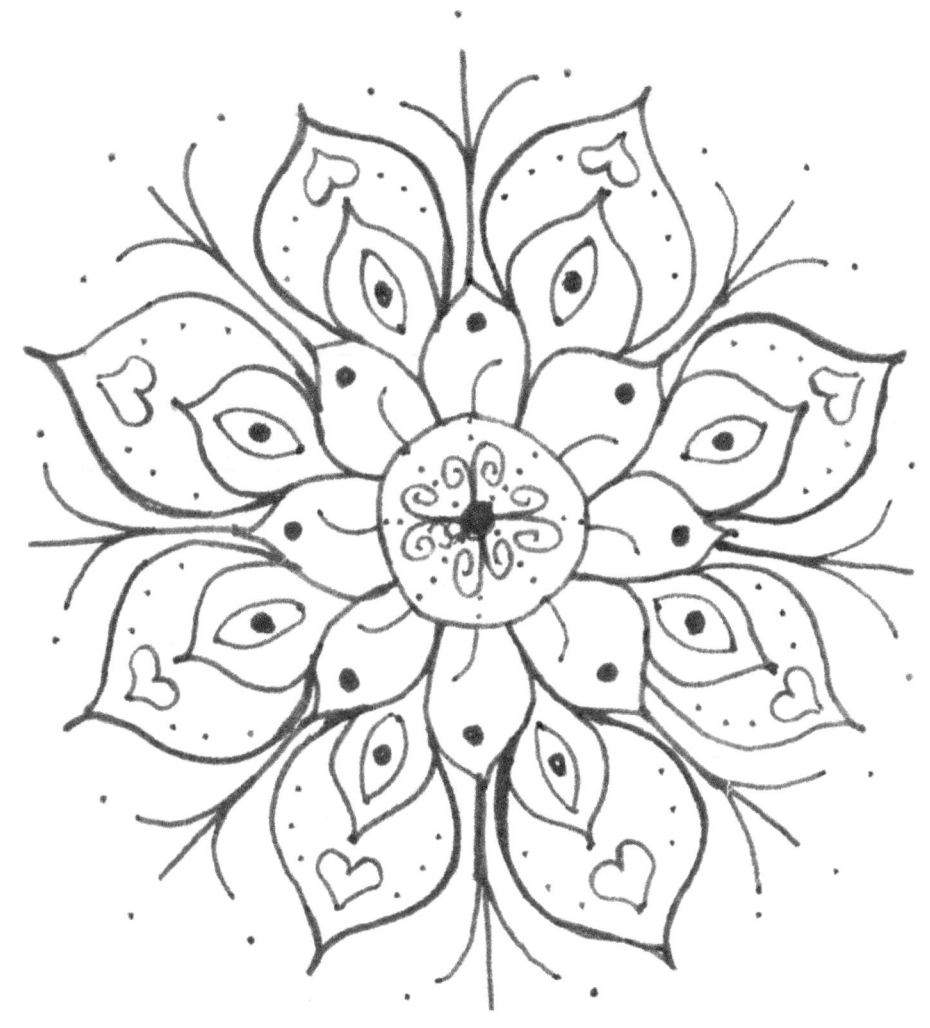

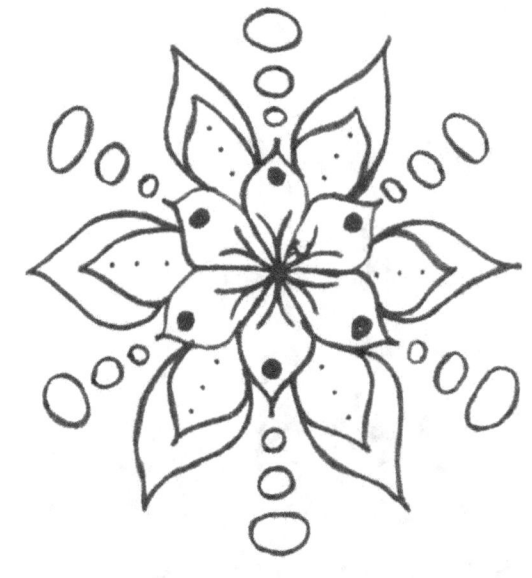

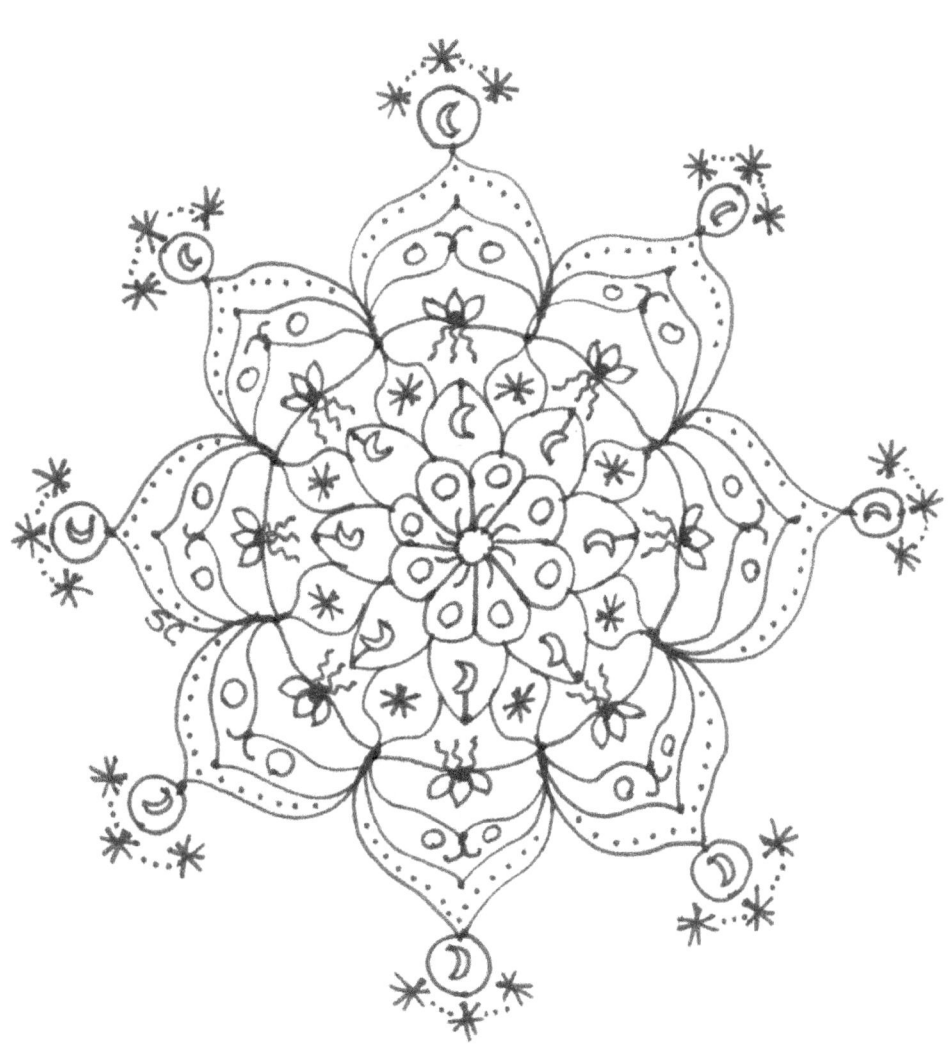

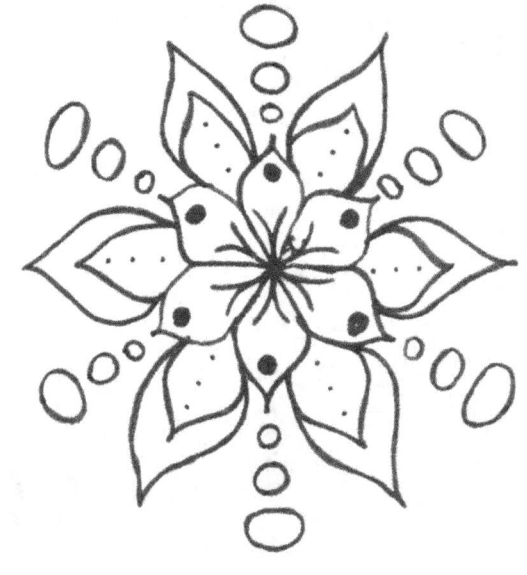

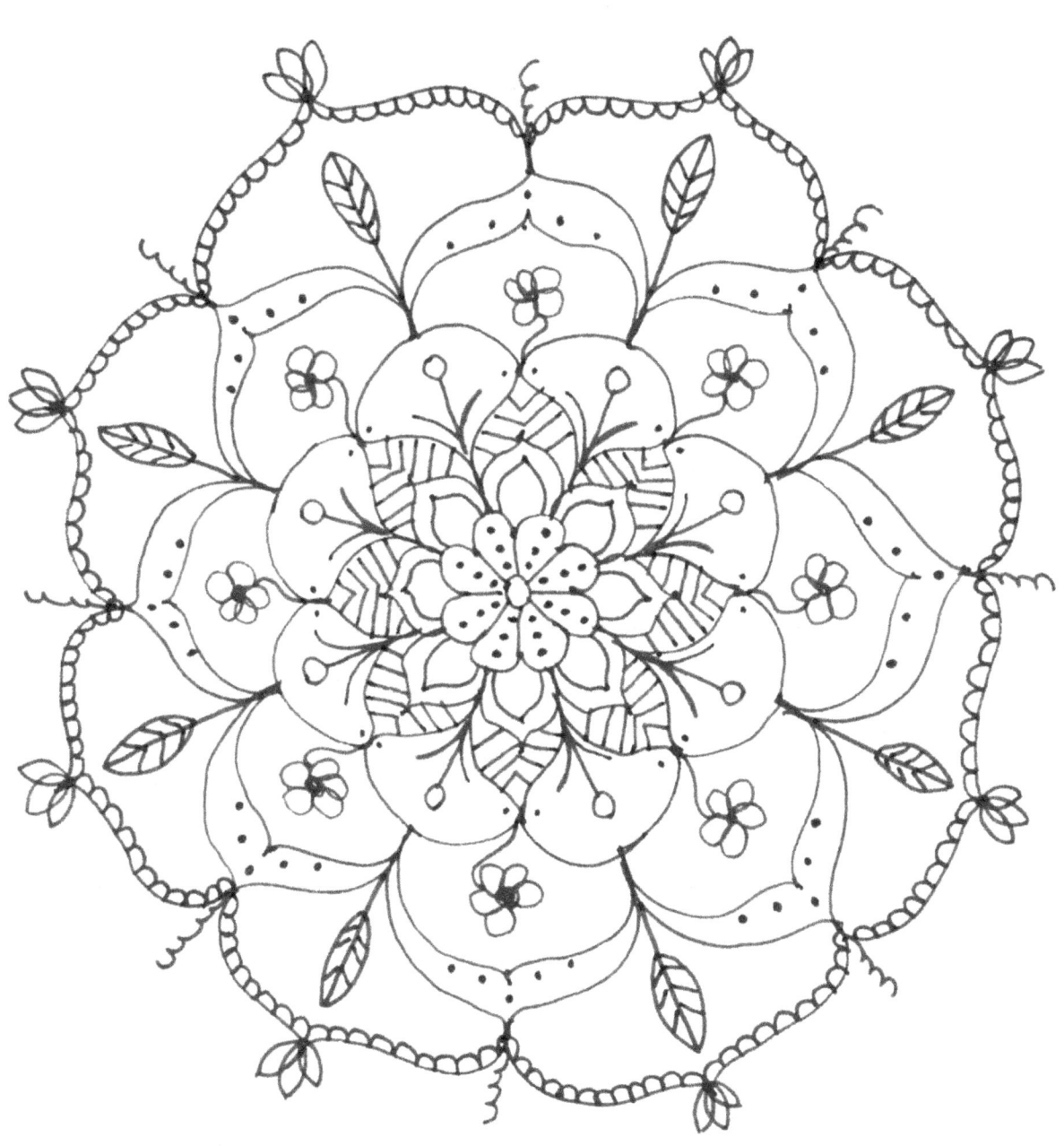

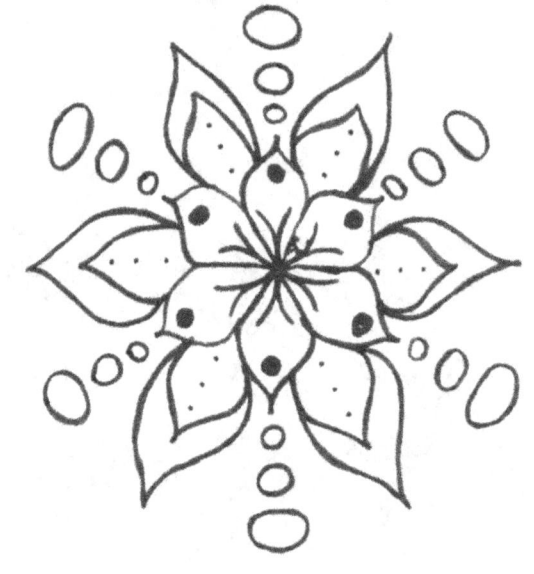

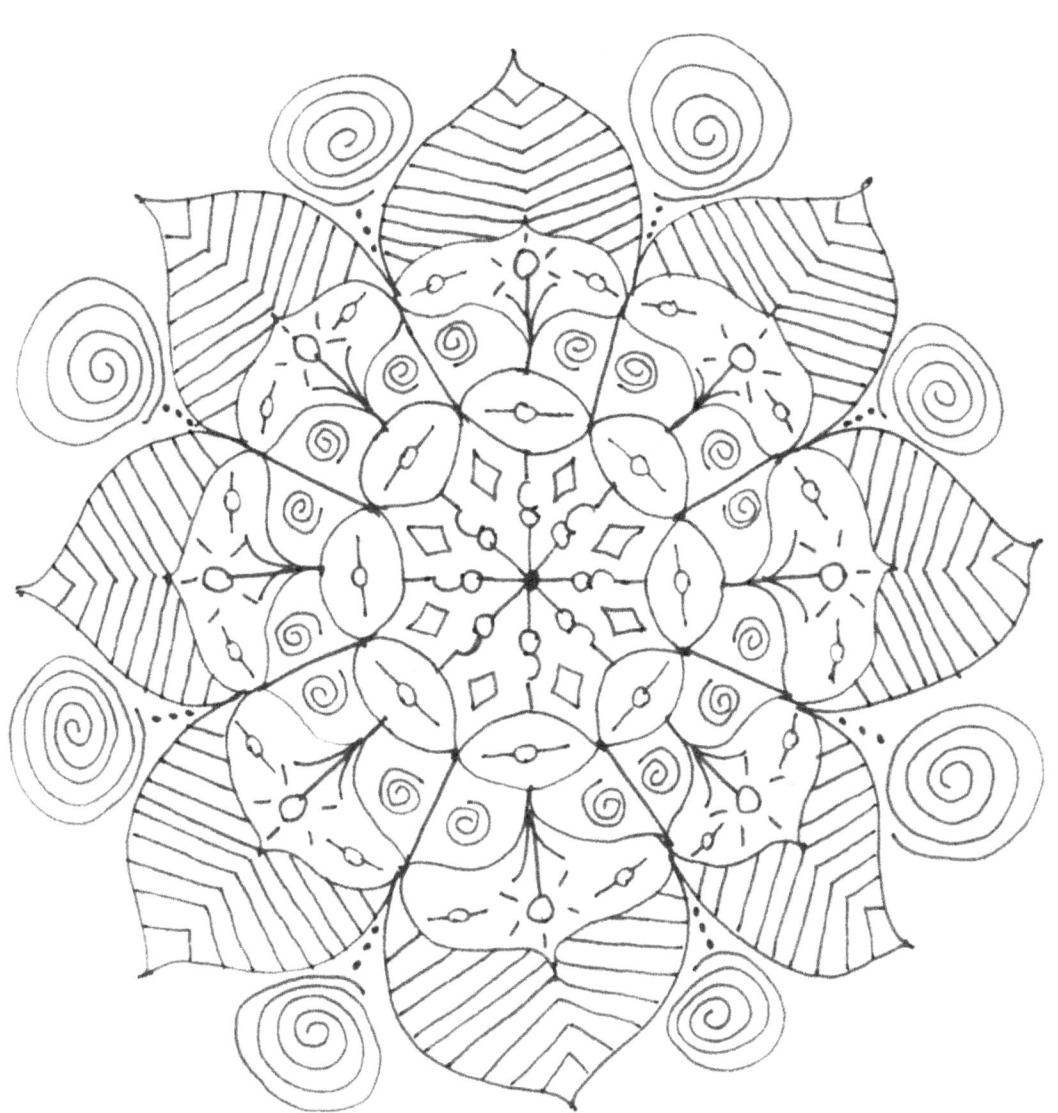

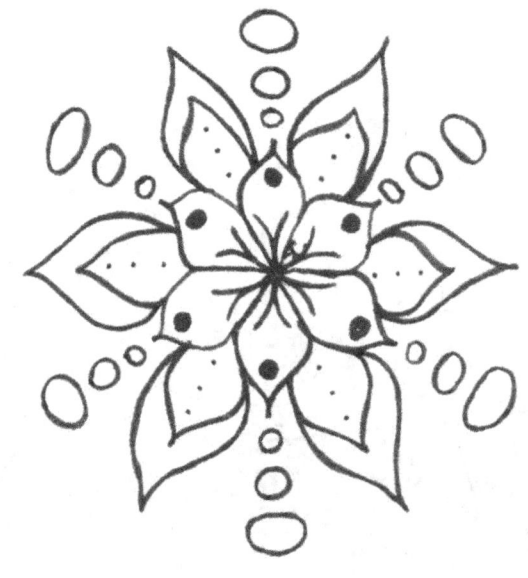

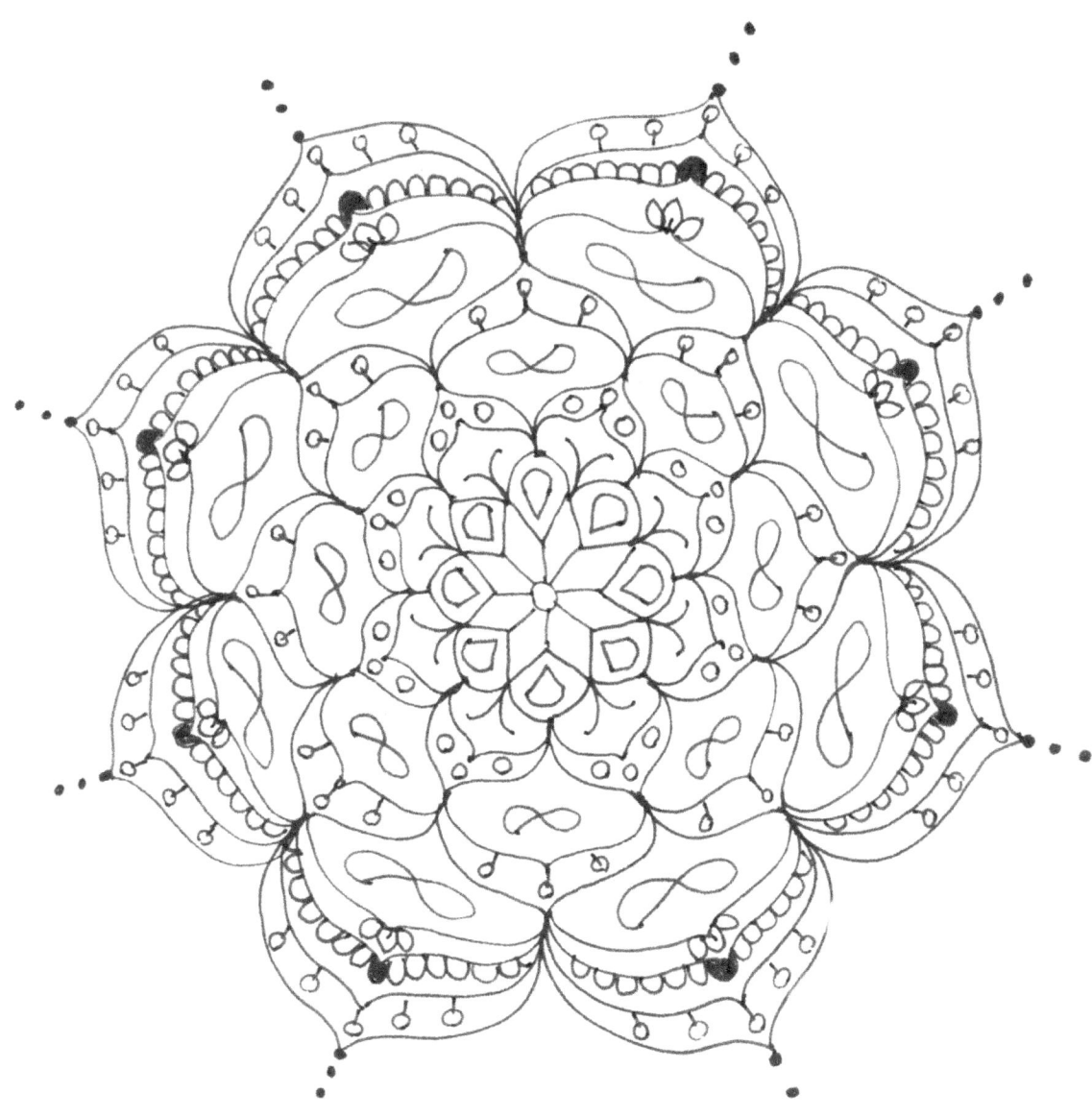

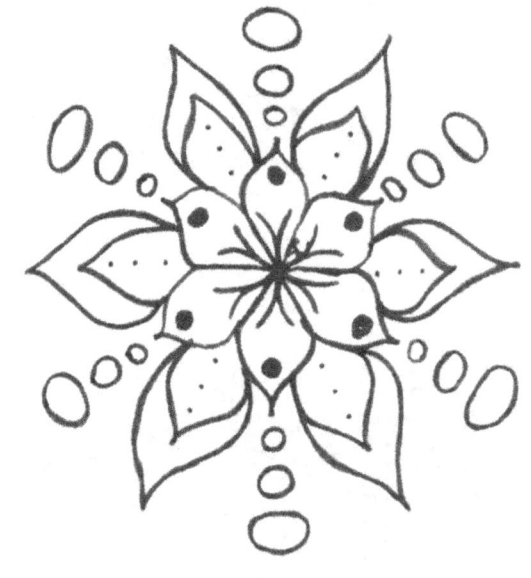

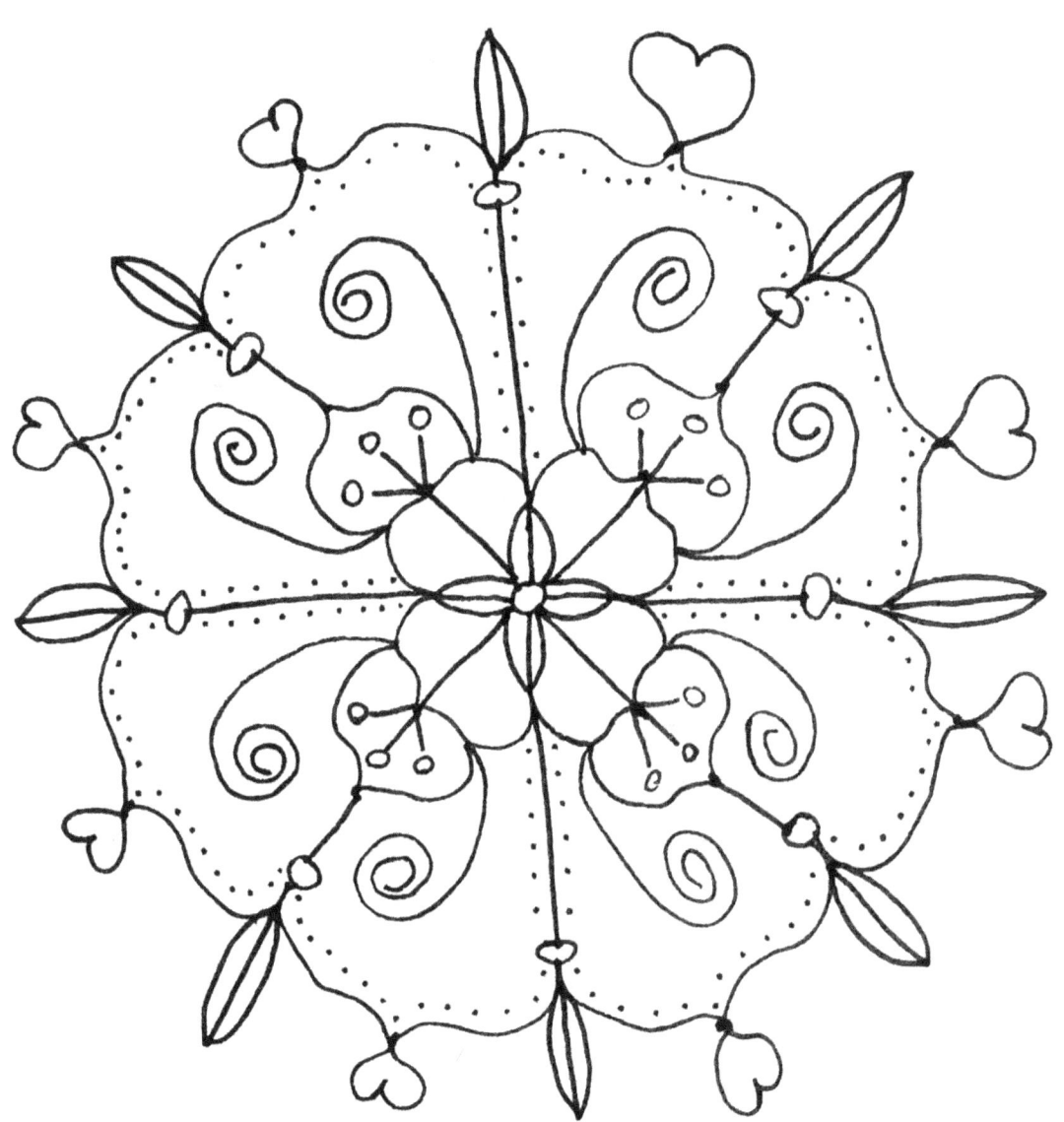

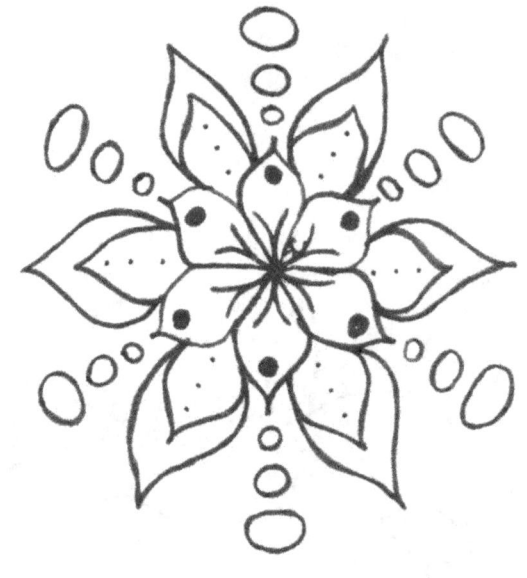

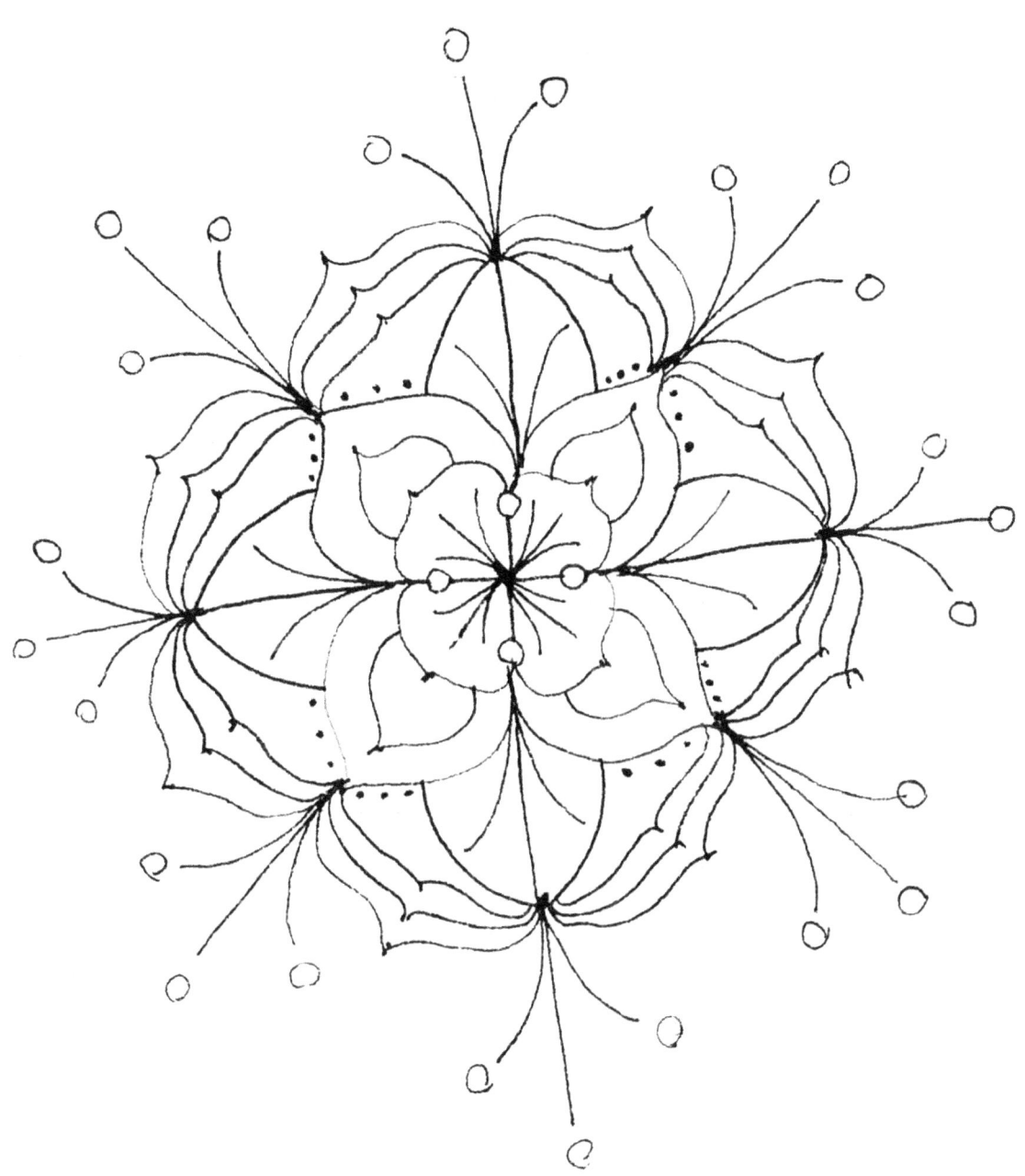

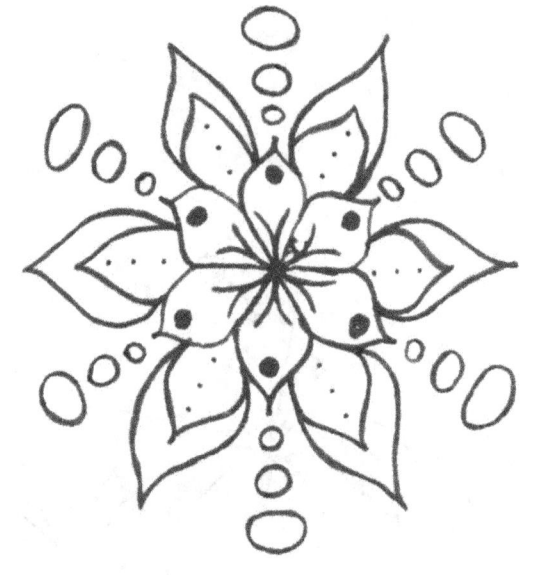

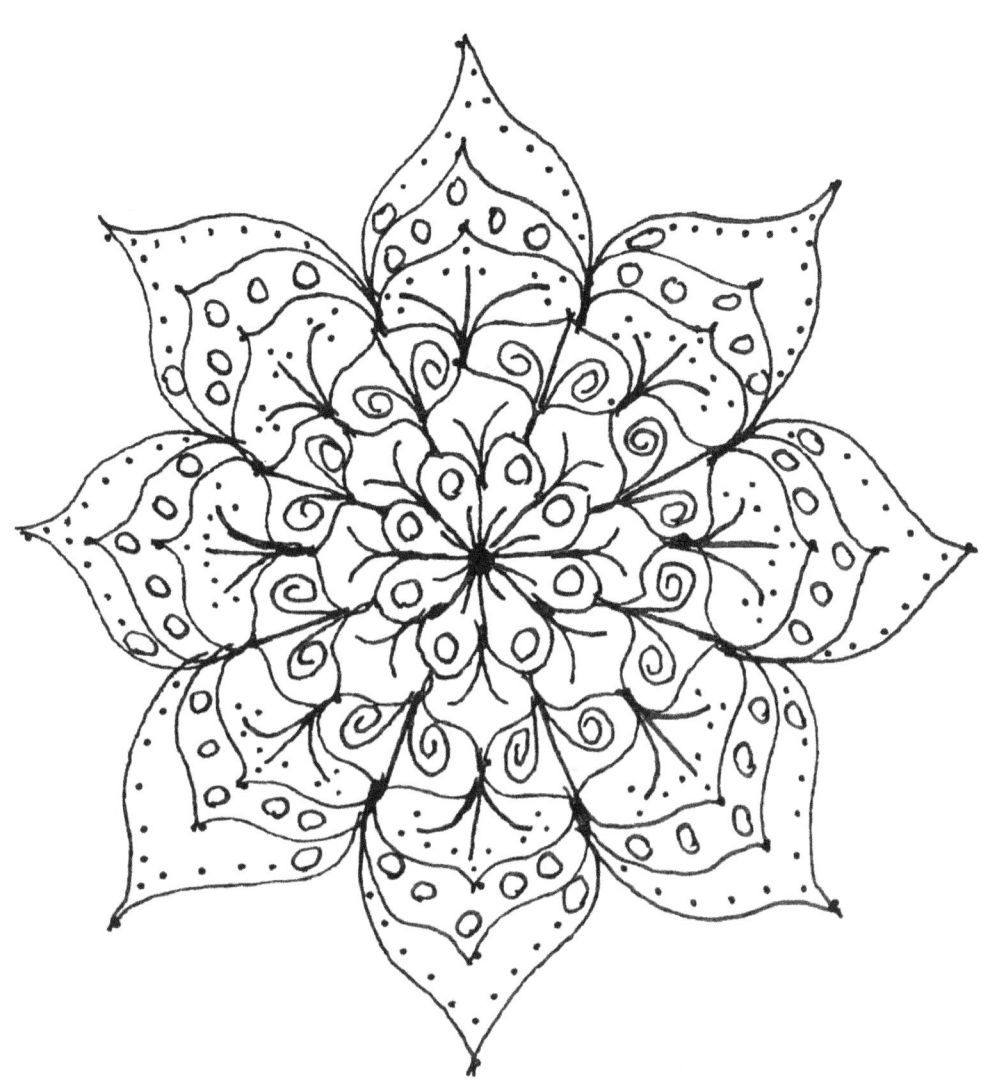

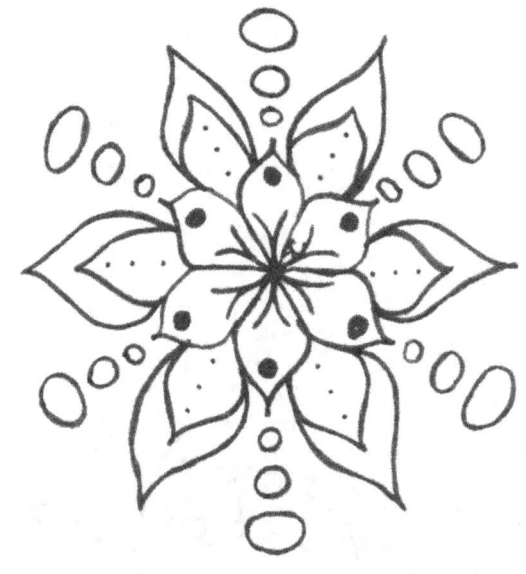

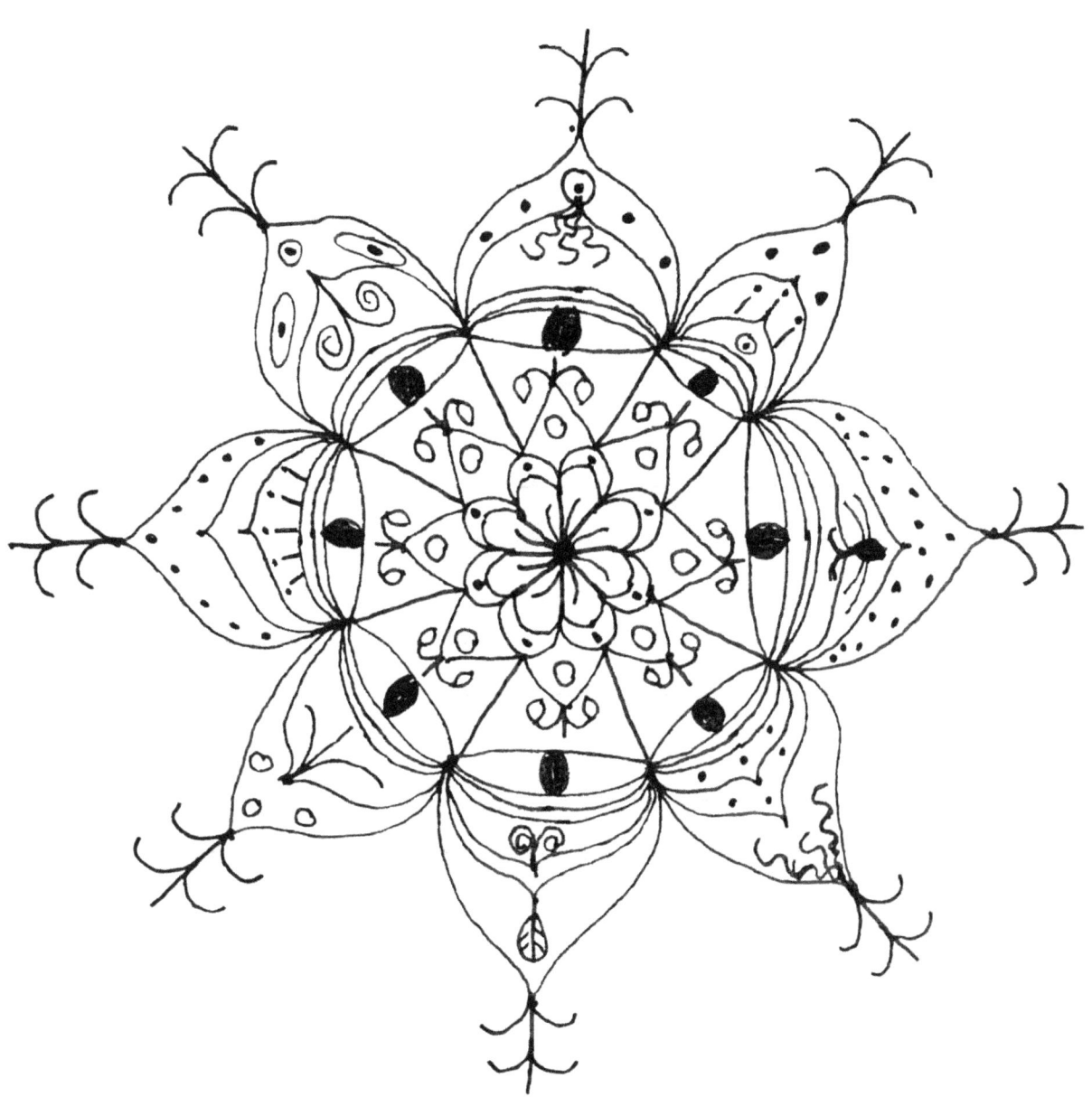

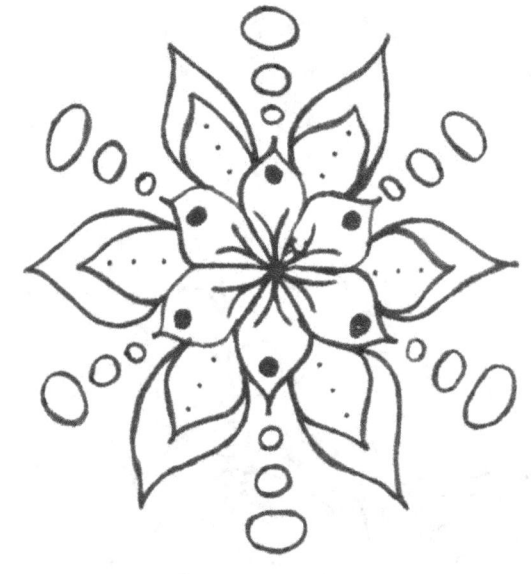

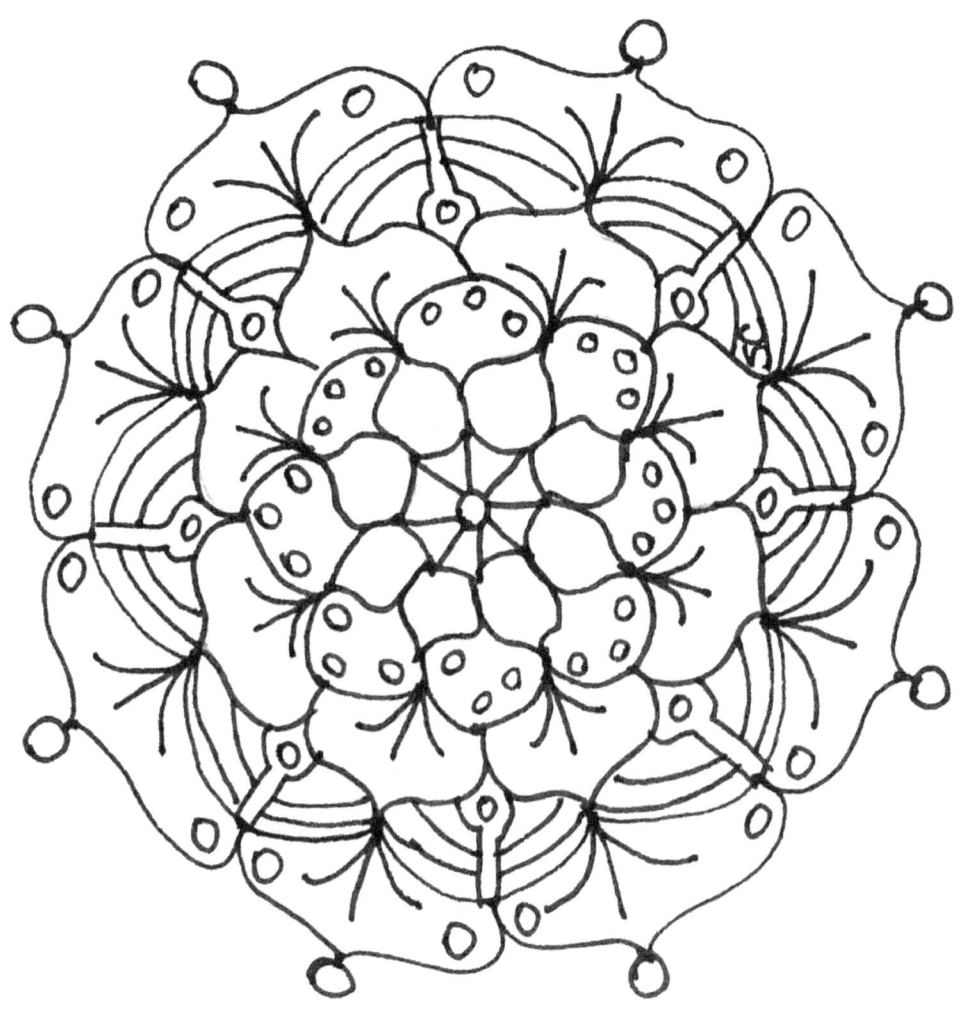

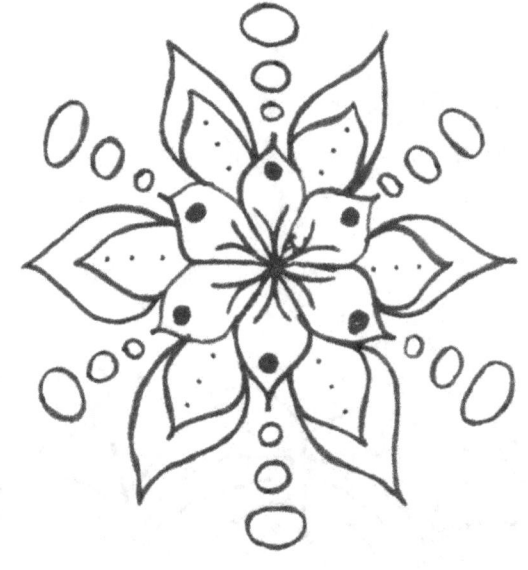

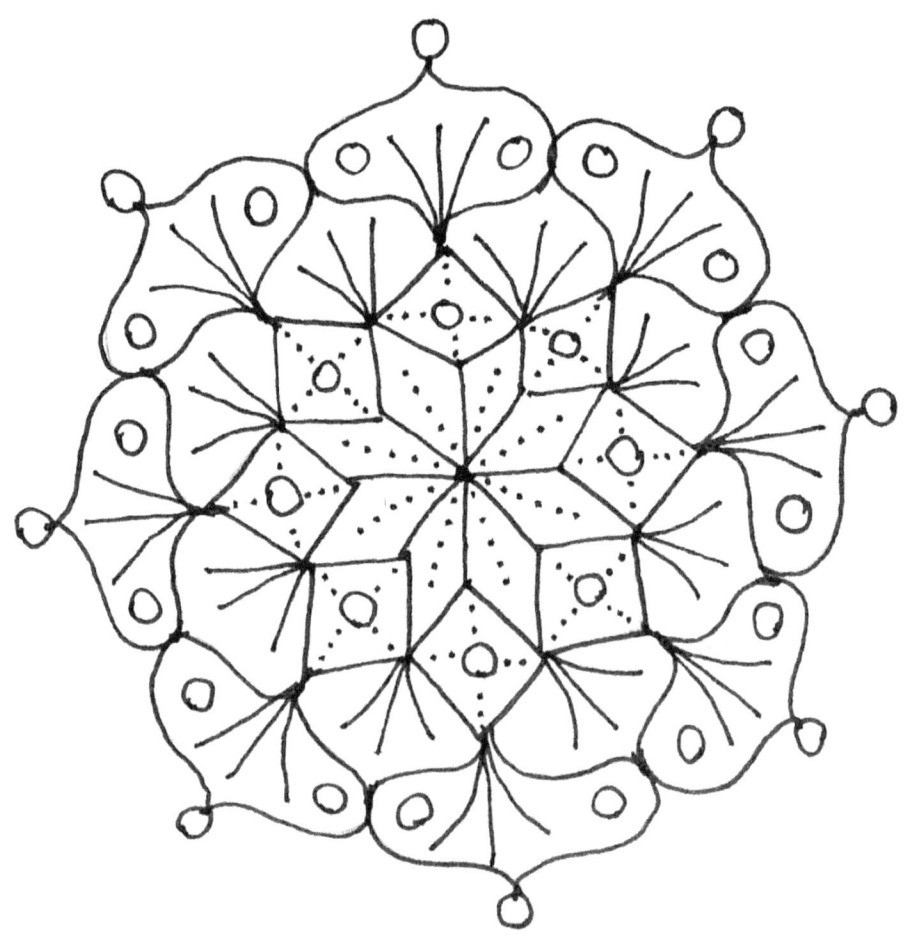

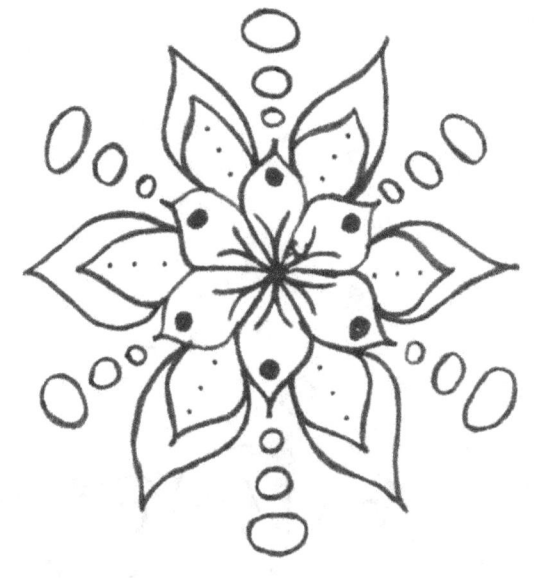

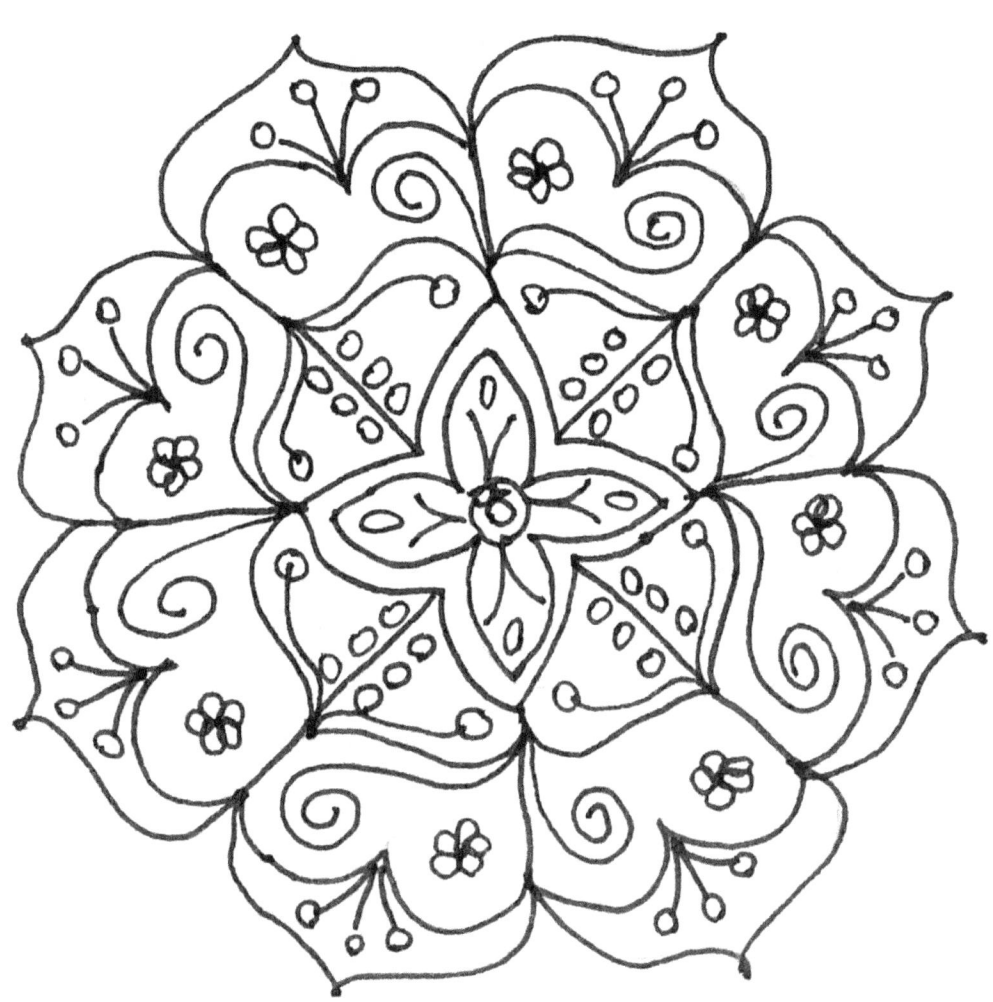

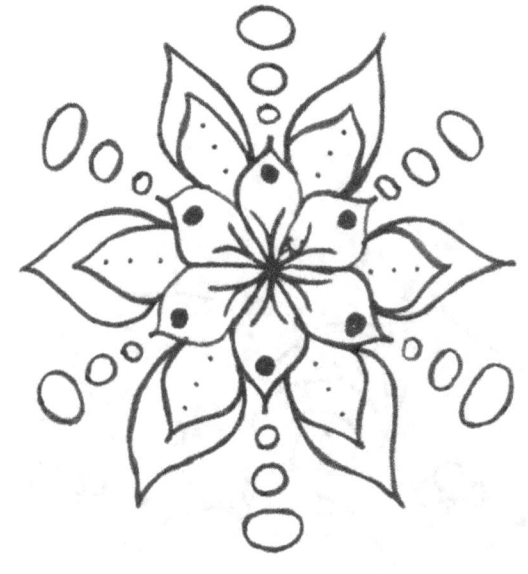

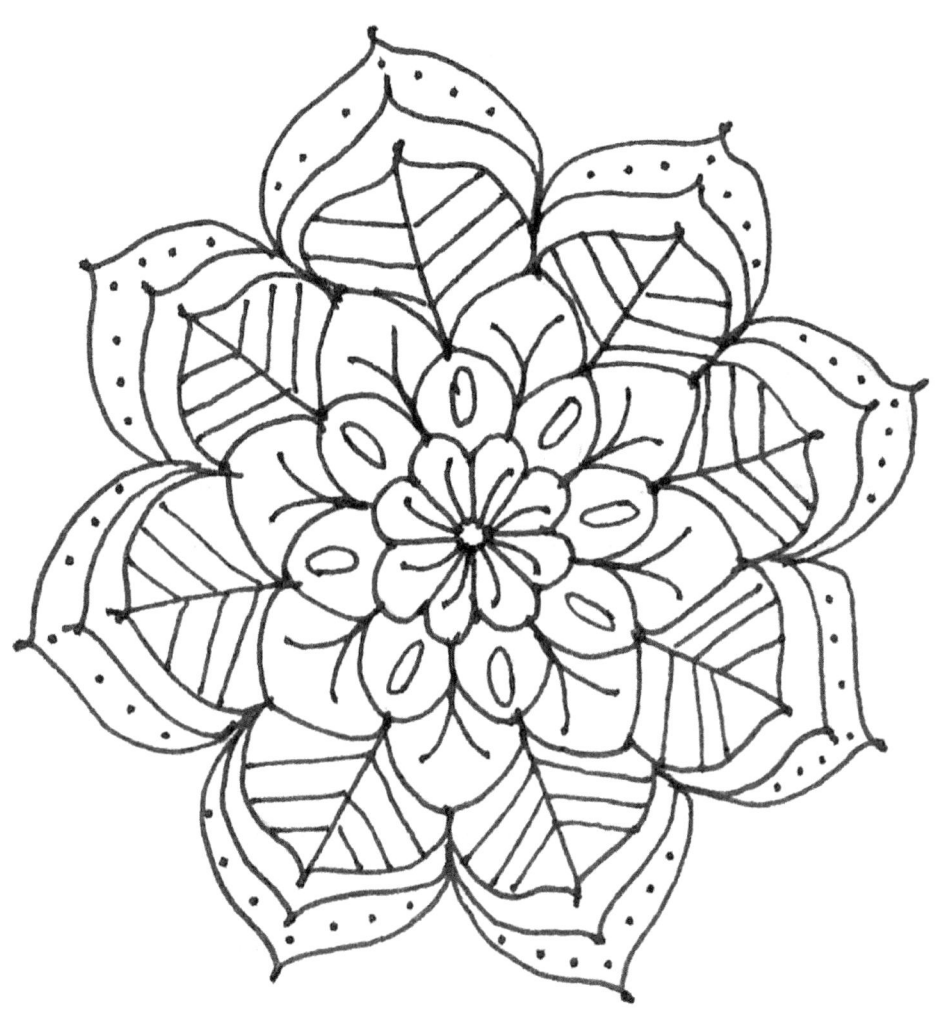

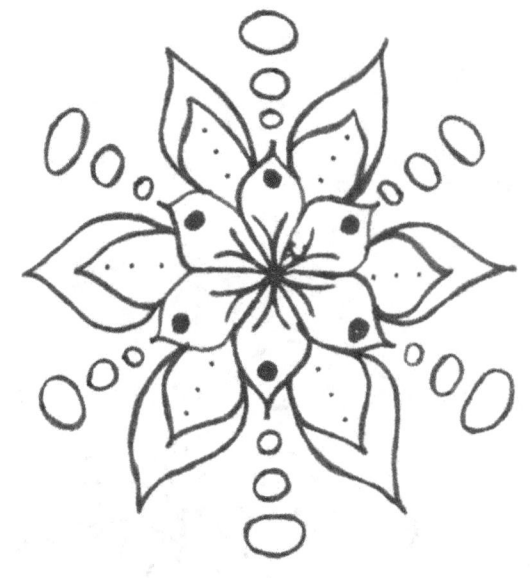

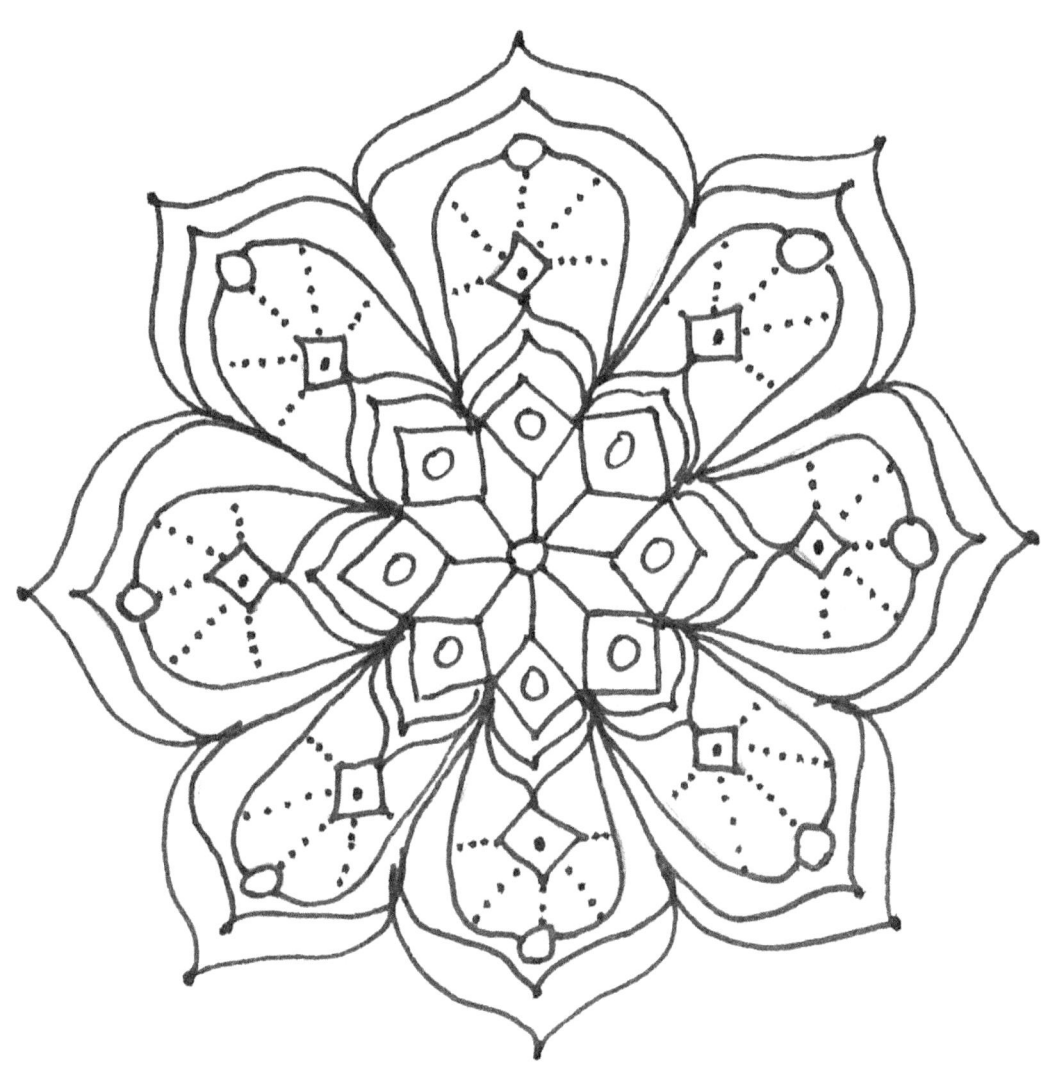

Discover more inspirational artworks at www.sacaveart.com

www.ingramcontent.com/pod-product-compliance
Lightning Source LLC
Chambersburg PA
CBHW080815220526
45466CB00011BB/3563